EXCHANGES ON LIGHT

Jacques Roubaud

exchanges

La Presse Iowa City & Paris

on light

translated by *Eleni Sikelianos*

Published in the United States by La Presse,
an imprint of Fence Books

La Presse/Fence Books are distributed by
University Presses of New England.
www.upne.com
www.lapressepoetry.com

Library of Congress Control Number 2008925086
Roubaud, Jacques
Exchanges on Light by Jacques Roubaud,
translated by Eleni Sikelianos
p.   cm.

ISBN 978-1-934200-02-5

1. French poetry. 2. Poetry. 3. Contemporary translation.

First Edition
10 9 8 7 6 5 4 3 2 1

This book was first published in French in 1990 by Éditions A.M. Métailié;
we would like to thank the publisher and the author
for graciously granting us permission to publish this translation.

EXCHANGES ON LIGHT

PROLOGUE

The Form of the Poem
or
Game with Light

Houses along the edge of the road, empty; nothing on the road;
no one.
    I to 0 light.
A lit window, only one; its rectangle.
    I all.
Night, and silence; and silence; silence.
    2-I light.
Rain stopped, no rain; wind died down, no wind.
    3-I.
Stars out, one after the other; no stars.
    4-I.
A lit window, only one, rectangle; the same rectangle.
    4-2.
Houses and nothing; behind, nothing; above, nothing; nothing.
    5-2.
A lit window, the only one; in the window's rectangle, a shape
begins.
    5-3.
Window dark
        blown out.
    game.

protocol

There are six voices:
1. Mr. Goodman
2. Basil of C.
3. Dennis Ps
4. Lewis de B.
5. John Ph.
6. William H.

FIRST NIGHT

MR. GOODMAN

I've asked you all to gather here for the next few evenings, just when the lamps are being lit, as the natural light is waning, leaving the outside world in darkness. Imagine that these windows open to the west, that right out there is the grass, the cultivated grass, of a park laid out by, say, Capability Brown, or perhaps Humphry Repton, with its orderly disorder of trees and, farther on, the low hills in the soft English distance.

But each of you might imagine another landscape, one beyond these windows facing us, one pierced by stars and lamps in which their lights meet, fight, trade, and leave even as we speak. It's of light that we speak, that you speak.

MR. GOODMAN

To begin:
No light, no world; and it's not just the world that's not, without light, but all that is, which is but light. Objects are worn-out light. The sum of all light is the world.

WILLIAM H.

Light is the boiling point of things.

BASIL OF C.

Light is an emanation from God; as emanation, it is an eternal process; it is not creation at each instant; for creation is *ex nihilo* and takes place in time, and light is natural while creation is a deliberate act.

10

JOHN PH.

Everything you have just trebly said is naught but this: the world is *luciforme a luce prima:* formed of light, derived from First Light. Light is the first bodily form. It is not objects but forms that are light, the only substance of the physical world that is nearly pure form, since all form is a form of light that manifests in the object that it informs.

DENNIS PS.

Light is what cannot be touched, untouchable even as lightning. The cause of all beings, itself nothing, being superessentially cut off from everything.

LEWIS OF B.

Be serious, let's not get carried away: when the sun, after hovering majestically on the horizon, sinks and suddenly disappears from sight, we understand that between this star and us exists a mode of communication that, without our having to touch it, brings its presence to mind. This mode of communication, which exercises itself over incommensurable distances and is transmitted via the eyes – this, and this alone, is light.

LEWIS OF B.

Let us not be poor in light, sunless. We are the Sun's debtors.

MR. GOODMAN

Yet all that rises in the park at this very instant: grass, trees, the distance, that which enfolds each form in a dark thought, like a finger of smoke, a dark dust, a red-blurred pollen, what all the things outside have in common, isn't that also light? And don't the laws of night vision permit us a slow substitution for the anterior, disappeared blaze of sun?

DENNIS PS.

If shadows had no light, we wouldn't see them. Darkness would be entire, eternal, and nil.

WILLIAM H.

Night you   come   the light   grows
on the   emptied slopes   of day   the
leaves will be   dark

JOHN PH.

Who can shed light on light?

The sun was not born to shed light. Light was made before the sun. The writings speak not of spreading light but of illuminating, by the very essence of light, rather than by the sun, which can only serve as a vehicle for something whose birth preceded its own.

BASIL OF C.

Light differs from shadow in that its existence cannot be separated from its essence; the essence of light is to purely exist; on the contrary, if it were of the essence of shadow to enter into composition with its existence, it would be impossible to perfectly conceive of the essence of shadow without the existence of shadows weaving in. Just as the essence of the number 2 would be destroyed if one tried to extract its unity, so the essence of shadow would be destroyed by removing shadows from the universe, by extracting the existence of shadow from its essence. But that's not possible. Yet it is possible to understand shadow's essence without seeing it, even without supposing that there are real shadows. Furthermore, if there were no distance between essence and existence in shadows, one could say that they existed thanks to their essence. But only light has this property.

LEWIS OF B.

Let's be serious. Why not try to prove that light is God, while you're at it?

JOHN PH.

I wouldn't say that. But why reject a metaphysics of light? It has
several divine traits, for instance, the begetting light and the splendor
begotten weave together and illuminate one another. Divinity does
that too.

13

M.G.

But isn't that what light is? There is light, and there are lights. Lights
are objects; light is arrow. The first change; the second does not.

WILLIAM H.

In the air
             light
                        tears out
      from earth   to dark
      and spits
               in the air
      night   rough to the verge
               of trees
                     in the earth

DENNIS PS.

Indeed. It's clear that each light tears itself away from night, but it is
also clear that in each shining thing, light in its essence and substance

is more brilliant still than its visible sheen, which is but the darkness and shadow of its full brilliance.

DENNIS PS.

These trees, this grass, these hills, like us, visible in the dying light, aren't they all as elusive as the inaccessible light, of which lights are but a shadow?

BASIL OF C.

Light, born of the first word of God, who fashioned it after his nature, instantly dispelled the dark. God separated light from darkness. Light and darkness are of incompatible natures, in perpetual opposition; between them is the largest interval, the longest distance.

WILLIAM H.

Night

you
came

the
lights
have grown
over

the grass, drained
the slopes
of

light, the
lights have

gone
dark

LEWIS OF B.

No light is dark; that doesn't make sense; there is more or less light, intensity, variable wave-lengths, that's all. Get serious.

MR. GOODMAN

I remember London in March, 1940, during the black-out. I was overcome, and still am, remembering; to see the city quietly give itself over to darkness (this was before the bombings), the way a countryside might, like the one we're looking at now from these windows, pushing itself into night. London humbly preparing herself in the twilight, the shutters shutting up windows, the rare passer-by hurrying towards home, the small medieval lanterns lighting up the subway entrances here and there. And darkness fell, and, with the diminishing gleam, noises rarefied, the sirens emerging from this dark mass one by one, as if night were painting it.

JOHN PH.

Configurations of objects make the state of light.

JOHN PH.

But of light or not light, from the former it is not possible to deduce, light or not light, the latter.

DENNIS PS.

Not-light is also the being of beings-of-light. We mustn't call them the simple reverse of perceptible light. If one reasons thus, one transforms them into their opposite, that is to say, into what is, in itself, darkness; instead of being that-which-manifests, that-which-illumines, they become only something manifested, the sign of a light other than that light that informs them. Contrary to what Aristotle said, all contingent realities, like the simple lights which appear on the hill, or those reborn in Mr. Goodman's memory of London, each accidental configuration, must be preceded by a more noble being: it's the illuminative exigency resting on the unconditional hegemony of illumination in relation to the object that it reveals.

M. GOODMAN

I was a child then. My mother lit the candles, I parted the black curtains, I leaned into the dark street near Russell Square.

BASIL OF C.

The smallest light, the most humble, the candle's, is all light, is Light.

LEWIS OF B.

You're confusing things again.

WILLIAM H.

```
    The lamps    evaporate              in the bottom
left rectangle       of the window                fill
with lights     from elsewhere      black and white
    from a light        the rectangle            of the
window              of lights       in black and white
        and the window        fill up       the lamps
            with lights    slowly and from elsewhere
```

WILLIAM H.

```
    The     lamps     evaporate    in    the     bottom
    left rectangle          of the window              fill
with lights from elsewhere          in black and white
        from a light      the rectangle          of the
window              of lights        in black and white
    and the window          fill up          the lamps
slowly with lights                  and from elsewhere.
```

JOHN PH.

Mental window, mental hands, mental lights, lights always already declared, by design reiterative.

LEWIS DE B.

Light doesn't turn the street corner.

DENNIS PS.

Light has already, while you were giving it boundaries, while you legislated the impossible, turned the corner.

BASIL OF C.

Light is not of time.

M. GOODMAN

Night is now complete, and neither the stars, nor time, are yet within the field of our conversation. It's time, according to our rules, to retire. We will reconvene here tomorrow at the same hour, if you will.

SECOND NIGHT

WILLIAM H.

Since it's my turn tonight to start these exchanges on light, I would like to read you a poem that I myself composed. It's an anagrammatism on the name of my friend Maistre Pierre Le Jumel, president of the Rouen parliament. It is, at the same time, a tribute to the spiritual beauty of light.

> In the light of the Mind and all that's right,
> In light of countenance, in light of grace,
> In light of our blood, in light of our race,
> In light of tongues speaking words grave and right,
> Hath our honor'd Father drench'd thee in light;
> As brilliant sun's clarity doth efface
> Every star in the Sky, on earth's face
> Your bright luster dims each mortal lords' sight.
> 'Round all twelve signs doth Phœbus his rays shine
> Thou, central father this cycle defines,
> Doth balance scales, thy court brimming so well
> With knowledge luminous by thine aiming;
> And thrice handsome from afar admiring
> HOW IN THEE HIS LIGHT STIRS, PIERRE LE JUMEL.

BASIL OF C.

If bodily beauty is based upon symmetry and the relation of parts to each other, and on the pleasing appearance of colors, how then, in light, whose substance is supple and made of like parts, does the notion of beauty obtain? Isn't it that light, as God testifies, possesses a balance based not on its specific components, but on the joy it occasions in those who look on it?

JOHN PH.

As far as I'm concerned, this beauty can be easily reduced to six points:

       i   light is metaphysical essence
      ii light is dynamic fact
     iii light is spherical impulse
    iv light is color at play
     v light is musical coronation
    vi light is rhythmic imperiosity

DENNIS PS.

Like a Praxitelis who liberates the latent statue from a block of marble, removing all impediments that mask the pure vision of the hidden form, so light, by heightening negatives, by steeping reverie in shadowy rays, reveals its hidden beauty, through *aphaeresis*, a negative-abstraction.

LEWIS DE B.

The only beauty conceivable in light is, as in all things, the beauty that comes to us from knowledge: to know what light is, to know how it moves, I ask no further beauty.   21

M. GOODMAN

Those are highly contrasting points of view. As for me, I would say: the beauty of light is its pain. I name light more than I see it. If I name light, I also name pain.

M. GOODMAN

But light isn't present in this naming, while pain penetrates my senses. If pain is not present in light, light does nothing but numb my senses.

WILLIAM H.

The lamps   evaporate   in the bottom   left
rectangle   of the window   fill up   with
lights from elsewhere   black and white from a
light   the rectangle   of the window   of
lights   in black and white   and the window
                fills *slowly* with lamps   with
lights   and from elsewhere.

In other words (I reiterate my previous affirmation), it's the most harmonious theories of light, the most experimentally verifiable, those richest in their explanations of phenomena apparently penetrated by the disparate power of natural events, that are the most esthetically accomplished. There is, to my mind, no other beauty in light, no more than there is poetry in a sunset. Light's beauty, all its beauty, can be found in Euclid or in Alhazen, in Huyghens, Descartes, or Newton, in Fourier, Einstein, De Broglie, or Feynmen, and not elsewhere, and there's more beauty in the latter than in the former; more and more beauty the more that light is known.

BASIL OF C.

When God said: "Let there be light," he banished sadness, filled the world with splendor and gave all beings, at once, a soft and laughing aspect. The sky, until then enveloped in darkness, leapt forth with the beauty our eyes still see there. The air blazed, or rather it mixed light in with its very substance, and in dazzlingly quick flashes, sent it in every direction to all of its edges.

DENNIS PS.

Let's leave light's motion out of our present discussion. For the beauty of light is not in its movement. It is rather in its essential quality, which is to *bring to sight*. Yet it isn't only that it makes natural things visible. That is but a secondary, relative, diaphanous beauty. The beauty of light – its black beauty – is its divine ipseity as a revelatory light.

No object is its gift; it is Light of *Lights,* at once light and darknesses (singular and plural), visible to grant sight, but itself invisible. Such is its beauty.

JOHN PH.

Light is the splendor and perfection of all bodily things.

JOHN PH.

It is therefore the principle underlying all beauty. Being the principle of color, light is the beauty and ornament of all that is visible. And being the principle of proportion, too.

M. GOODMAN

To call light beautiful, you have to be able to say: What light tells me is itself, but I can't say that, or rather, I can no longer say it. Unless light is seen as a super-resemblance.

DENNIS PS.

The beauty of light is the beauty of the dark.

Black Beauty.

24

Black beauty, which more than common light,
   Whose Power cannot bring colors back to life
   But those which darkness can again subdue,
Remain unvaried to the sight,

   And like an object equal to the view,
Are neither changed with day nor hid with night
When all these colors the world calls bright,
   And which old Poetry did so persue,

   Have vanished and perished with the night,
   That of their being there remains no mark,
Still you hold out, so entirely one,
   That we may know your blackness is a spark
Of inaccessible light, and only
   Our darkness can make us think it dark.

BASIL OF C.

Remove light, and all falls into darkness, unable to manifest its
beauty. Thus light is the basis of esthetic value, as ornamental as it is
constitutive of all visible things.

LEWIS DE B.

Black is rough; white, the luminous, is smooth.

LEWIS DE B.

The sea sparkles when split by oars. Black, thick, remains unmoved.

JOHN PH.

Beauty is the sum of all that truly exists in light.

BASIL OF C.

Why, in fact, seek a beauty that is the negative of or relative to light. Light is beautiful in and of itself; its nature is not constituted by number, weight, or measure. It is identified entirely and exclusively with the delectable quality under which it appears.

M. GOODMAN

The weight of light is to me like a stere of doors on ants.

WILLIAM H.

Just before light, time takes place, just after, beauty does; during light, light.

DENNIS PS.

Let us look for the beauty of light in its invisibility. Inaccessible to human sight is pure sun; we would only see it by holding an even brighter torch in our hand, and that is not possible; so we content ourselves with the indirect light of visible objects, but the beauty of light is not in them, in their beauty as created things, nor is it in light's absence from them; it is outside of their absence, not-other than light itself.

DENNIS PS.

For luminous beauty is not color, even if in color light is not-other than itself and even if light is not-other than color. Visible beauty is but a shadow of invisible beauty. The beauty of light, ever inaccessible, can only be approached in the ruby's flash, which is the incandescent point of light enclosed in a body; but it exceeds all color, all occurrence that the senses and imagination can apprehend; only intelligence can approach it, through understanding the movement of double negation.

LEWIS DE B.

I have nothing to say.

WILLIAM H.

In the air
                tears out
from earth
                to dark   the light
and spits it
                in the air
        night   rough   to the   verge
                of trees
        in the earth   the beautiful
            light.

JOHN PH.

Beauty is an episode of light.

M. GOODMAN

Light's beauty is its format, more than its form.

BASIL OF C.

It was God who first saw that light was beautiful. If a body's beauty is the result of symmetry and the pleasing appearance of colors, how can we, in relation to a simple and homogenous essence like light, maintain this constitutive notion of beauty? Won't light's symmetry show itself less in its parts than in the pleasure and sweetness of its sight? The evening star is the most beautiful of stars, not because its parts form a pleasing proportion, but because of the enchanting, lively brilliance it offers the gaze. Moreover, when God proclaimed the beauty of light, he was not thinking of charming our eyes; he was foreseeing its future benefits, for there were no eyes yet to judge its beauty.

BASIL OF C.

Light is the very substance of beauty.

DENNIS PH.

God saw that light was beautiful, you say. I say God saw that light was beautiful, and light was created. The beauty was in negating not-light. It is there in what is not-other than light, but is not light itself, from which it proceeds.

M. GOODMAN

Pure beauty; there is no beauty purer than the repetition of light, which loses itself.

LEWIS DE B.

I've said it: nothing to say that I haven't already said on this subject.

JOHN PH.

The necessary condition for all beauty, as Mr. Goodman has more or less said, is the loss of identity, the instant of this loss, the past of this loss, its grief. Behind its game of return, corroborated by multiplicity (hell), light is that constant that cuts across fact; the law of beauty is what permits a movement from symphony to score, a showing without telling; light is that condition; it is the condition of showing; it alone says without saying. And yet, to say of two visible things that they are identical would be absurd, and to say of any visible thing that it is identical to itself is saying nothing at all. Identity only exists in invisibility. The beauty of light must leave this world, leave the object, substance of the world, must lose itself in the least state of things, to give itself over to invisibility, where light's own identity is rendered possible by super-resemblance. That's why the object (not objects) is colorless, stateless: before light's predication, which grants it access to the state of thing and therefore to representation, the object is beauty's pure, empty scaffold; it only achieves that state by being named. It is light that names it, that draws itself out of the object into itself; only then is there beauty.

Night

you
came

the
lights
have grown
over

the grass, the slopes
emptied
of

light, the
lights have

arrived in the absence
of light

dark
of light lost

of light that was
beautiful

THIRD NIGHT

BASIL OF C.

Over the past two nights, we have considered, first the *nature* of light, then its *beauty*. Tonight we will focus on its *movement*. You will agree that light's mandate issues from the divine. Which is why, again, I seek the answer to the question of light's motion in the word of God. For God said, "Let there be light"; he didn't say, "Light will be" or "Let light come to pass." At the exact moment God spoke, light rushed through the ether, through the sky, and, in an instant without extension, lit all the world, the North as well as the South, the Orient as well as the Occident. As soon as God's order was heard, it was instantaneously executed.

JOHN PH.

Light is Creation's first corporeal form; one could call it corporeality itself. The problem solves itself so easily if you simply hold this axiom in mind.

DENNIS PH.

Visible light, descending light, is essentially slow, although to our blind eyes it seems infinitely quick.

LEWIS DE B.

I maintain that light, being a body (its body being an emanation issuing from luminous bodies) appears first in the intermediary space between earth and sky, and then travels to us in a motion so rapid it escapes our notice.

M. GOODMAN

I have trouble grasping both its instantaneity and its ubiquity. It seems to me that an infinitely quick light would be motionless.

WILLIAM H.

The paths,
              cleared through the dark,
                                        of light
    are facts.

WILLIAM H.

The paths, cleared through the dark, of light
that goes without saying because we know
all light goes, clearing its way, through the dark.

BASIL OF C.

Light doesn't clear its way through the dark, it dissipates it, annihilates it; but it crosses air, and air is a substance so subtle and diaphanous that light needs not the least instant to cross it. Just as it brings sight suddenly to the objects that strike it, and just as, without any interval at all, with a rapidity thought cannot conceive, it receives light's streams in all its extremities. Light makes the ether more pleasant and the waters more limpid, and the latter, not content simply to receive its luster, send back light's reflection, throwing off bright sparks. Light's voyage is instantaneous because it is obeying divine order, but also because it is, by nature, determined to leave darkness no means, not even temporary, of survival. In the presence of light, there is no dark.

M. GOODMAN

Then is emptiness dark? Doesn't Heron of Alexandria tell us that if there were no void, light could not make its way through water? He goes on to say that if this fluid, like air, had no pores, a vase of water would overflow whenever light struck its surface, which it doesn't do.

JOHN PH.

Yes it does, with light.
But I would put it more like this: light, by its very nature propagates in all directions in such a way that a point of light instantly produces a sphere of every dimension unless an opaque body interrupts it and deforms some of them. Matter's extension into the four dimensions (I don't exclude reversible time) is concomitant to corporeality; non-luminous matter is, by contrast, substance without true dimension, therefore it can't multiply or move by itself in any dimension at all. Light alone has the power to multiply and propagate instantly in all

directions. I'd say it is the agent, par excellence, of the creation of all dimensions.

LEWIS DE B.

For the moment, I'd simply like to point out that a movement that takes an infinitely small amount of time is not an instantaneous movement; an imperceptible interval is not an instant of no duration. Reread Alhazen.

DENNIS PS.

Although moving in an instant that is (because of our own slowness) imperceptible, visible light is essentially slow. For it doesn't emanate directly from an absolute luminous core, but from a dark body (dark like ours, like all material bodies). A body, a dark body, is a sponge for light; it absorbs real light and adulterates it. Heated like the stars, it goes from red to white, but the glow it emits, which we call light, is only a distortion of the true light it has swallowed and which we force it to give back.

DENNIS PS.

True light clarifies matter in its subtle, ethereal state by acts of light, incandescences of *mundus archetypus,* of the world of figures and forms. Yes, its motion is instantaneous; yes, its speed is infinite and in a way that escapes you because it's not a matter of simultaneity but of a sequence in no time.

WILLIAM H.

Any light can potentially successively disperse
that that it is, which is
light

LEWIS DE B.

Let's get this straight: simultaneity and sequentiality are two attributes
of light that our friends Dennis Ps. and William H, following their
own theories, agree to recognize in light (for reasons which, I must
humbly say, escape me); however, there's a well-accepted notion
that reconciles this contradiction – the Ray of Light. Rays of Light are
the minimal units; individually, they're sequential, and collectively,
they're simultaneous. We know that light is organized in parts that
are both successive and simultaneous because you can stop arriving
light at a given moment and let light pass a moment later at the same
spot; simultaneously, you can stop light at one spot and let it flow
through at another. The portion of Light that is stopped cannot be
the same as that which passes. Let us call Rays of Light those minimal
Lights that can be stopped apart from the total Light, and can be
propagated singularly, that act or are activated in ways the rest of
light cannot act or endure.

BASIL OF C.

Let's say, for example, we see the sun rising. Clearly, our gaze can't
reach it without traveling across all the space occupied by sky and air
between it and us. Is anyone really capable of grasping that distance?

Yet our gaze or our visual ray will certainly never manage to cross the air above the sea if it doesn't first cross the air above the earth, the entire distance from where we stand to the sea's shore. And if other lands interrupt our line of sight, our sight can't leap across the air stretched out over these far-off lands without first crossing the middle space. Let's now suppose that there's nothing left beyond that but ocean. It occupies an immense expanse, but regardless of its size, the visual ray must cross the air above it and whatever else may lie beyond in order to reach the sun. And although I might have used the terms "before" and "after," didn't our gaze cross all these spaces instantly?

JOHN PH.

Light was the first form created from primal matter, and that's why by nature it is infinitely multiplied, spreading uniformly in infinite directions. But material extension cannot be achieved by a finite multiplication of light because, as Aristotle showed in De Caelo et Mundo, the finite multiplication of an entity could not create quantity. But an infinite multiplication could. So light, simple in itself, multiplied infinitely, created finite matter (and is still creating it). Creator of finite time, itself infinite, it endlessly superinfinitizes within the confines of the universe, creating further infinities, which are to infinity what infinity is to the finite.

M. GOODMAN

I once read a series of objections to the idea that luminous movements are infinite. If I remember correctly, it went something like this:

"a. what the instant is to the point, the point is to the line, which is why, through exchange and permutation, what the instant is to the point, time is to the line. Passing through a point occupies an instant, and so traveling a line requires time. Therefore light, crossing a segment of space, however short, travels in an interval that is not void of time;

b. light travels faster in a straight line than in an oblique one, but both the fastest and the slowest require time (this argument seems weak to me);

c. no force acts instantaneously, as a greater force would then have to act in less than time;

d. a before and an after in space assumes a before and an after in time;

e. Instantaneity ensures that light lights an infinite number of places at the same time. It would be God."

M. GOODMAN.

And I read another argument somewhere that led to the same conclusion:

"light is a transmutation; all transmutation is instantaneous unless it encounters resistance; resistance assumes a contrary, but light has no contrary; it only has loss."

The loss of light is darkness; the darkness of a dark body is this darkness. It is not the Dark of the more-than-luminous shadow.

Light has its own contrary (the photon, that blind approximation of light has its antiparticle, which is itself), black Light, which infinitely exceeds visible light; that is why your philosopher's argument will not do. Physical dark is non-light. Dark Light is non-non-light, an entirely different thing.

JOHN PH.

Rarefaction is not loss. As I said, because light has spread matter by its infinite self-multiplication in all spacio-temporal directions in infinitely multiplied spherical layers, the outer edges (of each infinitude— infinites being heirarchized) are more rarefied than the inner layers, and closer to the primordial point of light. And since the farthest layer is the rarest, it gives the illusion of emptiness.

WILLIAM H.

Hell is a palace of strange architecture
Shut in on all sides by the Stygian tributary,
A theatre in which Pluto manifests his cruelty,
Where one feels in death eternity's factor.
The foundation is coal, arches of rapture,
Cool shadows run hot, flames rise icebound,
Here howls and tears never resound
Where terror and rage govern torture.

'Tis here the arrogant angel on high's sworn,
Where men's souls languish for having ignored
He unto the world so perfectly born.
But the greatest torment Hell can trace
Is the loss of the visage of the Lord,
Since Heaven is the instant of his face.

BASIL OF C.

I'm going to approach the problem differently to bring you to the truth. Nature loves everything that is useful and good for living things, and strives to create that. Because living things find it useful to see quickly, nature made sure that the visual flow would arrive at sight's object as quickly as possible. Now, since the fastest motion is the instantaneous, the visual flow instantly reaches sight's object.

LEWIS DE B.

Right. And crème caramel was created simply to be confused with crème brulée! Let's be serious: as soon as the Sun appears on the horizon, Earth's upper hemisphere is instantly and completely illuminated. How does that happen? Just as when you move the end of a long, taut rope, the whole rope moves instantly because all its parts are united, and the first moves the next and so on; so luminous energy moves, since all the bodies in the cosmos immediately touch one another.

And I'd go further than that. Please follow me through this thought experiment.

No doubt at some time or other, you've found yourself walking over rough ground at night without a torch, so that you had to use a stick to find your way, and you must have noticed that you could feel the various objects that you encountered through the intermediary of the stick and that you could even identify them – trees, rocks, sand, water, grass, mud, whatever. True, these perceptions are a bit confused and dim to those who aren't used to it, but think of people who were born blind and have used this method their whole lives, and you'll find it so perfect and precise that you might almost say they see with their hands or that their sticks are organs of some sixth sense given them in place of sight. To make the analogy, I ask you to consider that light, among what we call luminous bodies, is nothing more than instant motion, an infinitely quick and infinitely animated action that arrives at your eyes through the intermediary of the air and other transparent bodies, just as the response or resistance of everything that this blind person encounters passes into his hand through the mediation of the stick.

M. GOODMAN.

But don't we find ourselves once again, by following an idea quite philosophically distant from that of our friend Dennis Ps, faced with the notion that hidden behind visible light (which is of a finite speed, as everyone knows) is a parameter light that is non-local in essence and able, at the quantum level, to instantaneously affect the farthest reaches of the universe?

BASIL OF C.

Give that power back to God.

DENNIS PS.

Let's retrace the steps of the illuminative sequence. Have the intelligence to understand that this is what permits intelligences to see themselves as shared light and to see the theophanic light available to them. Don't confuse the uniqueness of absolute light with the multiplicity of lights, which is only dispersion and darkness.

WILLIAM H.

Dissipation, diversity, signs of death, forced plurality.

JOHN PH.

Light is not the flow of a body, like water, but a wave, like sound.

JOHN PH.

That was confirmed by Roger Bacon. On the other hand, Pythagoras saw it as fine particles sent like numerable messages by luminous bodies.

LEWIS DE B.

Having considered this problem all my life, I have come to the conclusion that no one has yet discovered a way to elucidate the relationship between waves and particles.

WILLIAM H.

            in the grass
                  grains waves
                        of light
                  attach   the earth
                  to black
                  and spit them
            in the grass   the night   real to the
      edges
                        of trees
            beneath the earth

M. GOODMAN

Newton attempted to synthesize the granular concept and the undulatory concept. He realized that light came in grains and thought it was conveyed by an undulation, at least while passing through matter, and that this undulation acted upon the grains, causing the corpuscles of light to pass regularly and alternately through "fits of easy transmission" and "fits of easy reflection." Arriving at the surface separating the two zones, the grain of light will pass easily if it's in a fit of easy transmission but will be bounced back if it's in a fit of easy reflection.

DENNIS PS.

God desired the finite transmission of visible light. God has 700,000 veils of light and shadow; if he took them off, the radiance of his Face would reduce all who encountered his gaze to ash. These veils are the ensemble of all perceptible and imperceptible universes, and all these worlds exist inside man, visible to as many eyes. One sometimes opens them in dreams, and parts of them sometimes fall on their own into memory.

BASIL OF C.

Luminous bodies were created in one fell swoop by the divine power and, without any local disturbance, were instantly applied to the air capable of receiving illumination. And light, the divinely inspired negation of the rule of the non-distributive divisibility of the All, arrived in an instant in every sky.

FOURTH NIGHT

JOHN PH.

...nevertheless you must admit that we see not light, but images. Where do they come from? I say that these elusive figures and pictures are emitted by objects and shine forth from their surfaces. Let's call them, by approximation, skin or bark, for each has the shape and appearance of the object, whatever it may be, from which it wanders, invisible in darkness, yet visible in light, in space.

DENNIS PS.

Don't equate images with angels. Images are not angels. Their substance is neither pneuma nor fire; Origen says that the substance of angels is like ether, incorruptible, perfectly pure, a dazzling light. By nature, angels are not visible to humans, not even to those who try to see them. Though they may condescend to show themselves to those whom God has illuminated with the light of knowledge.

LEWIS DE B.

If that were so, then whether angel or image, light would be a physical discharge flowing from the luminous object at a finite speed, or else a series of transformations in the transparent medium needed for its transmission. But it is in fact neither process nor movement; it's more a state and quality that the medium acquires instantaneously, just as all parts of a body of water freeze simultaneously when struck by winter.

Yesterday I read something in Buridan that seems germane to the present discussion: "In the natural order, light (*lumen*) does not reach a thing at once and entire through the air, but rather bit by bit, in continuous time, step by step. Imagine a dark house as it lights up. The illumination comes either from the approach of a luminous body, such as the setting sun, or by the removal of an obstacle, say, by the opening of a window, or even, if you like, by the arrival of angels or images of things. Yet in all of these cases, the illumination of air in the house, in this room where we're standing, is an event in time, for either luminous bodies and images approach the openings offered by the dark house on the hill, making the internal light slowly more and more intense, or the obstacle blocking them disappears in a succession of moments in time, creating the same gradual increase of light and images."

WILLIAM H.

Shadowy images, like a snake's skin, or a scent, or a mist, detach from things and drift off. Many objects emit abundantly and not only from their depths but also from their surfaces, giving off color. This is particularly true of the yellow, red, and green veils that, stretched across our vast theaters, float and wave along masts and drapes. Below, the gathered audience in the stands, the décor, the stage, and the august rows of senators are tinted and tinged with their shifting reflections. And the higher and narrower the theater's walls, the more the objects are bathed in these pleasing colors of the day's rarefied light.

BASIL OF C.

An image is a birth from the radiation of divine light. All birth is a kind of passage, a journey, a transmission of the essence of the thing giving birth to that which is born, and this is accomplished by the passage itself, and what is accomplished is the becoming of what is being born, in which the being arrives and is transmitted by that which gives birth to it.

BASIL OF C.

And as with any birth, production, or realization, and particularly with images born of light, we must conceptualize and distinguish four aspects: – the being to be born, in some way contained within the being that gives birth to it – the movement or transmission that light, from its core, evokes in the image it gives birth to – light's being as a site of possibilities and departures, from which the image to be born detaches – and that which is to be born (the image) as a site and goal attained, to which being is given and arrives. These four things are present in all birth in the instantaneity of an instant and the singular solitude of time because, as I said before, what gives birth and what is born are together in all birth, in the same instant of time, that which makes and that which is to be made, light and image, image and light.

JOHN PH.

I maintain that there are images in the shapes of bodies. Formed of impalpable tissue, they fly through space, and their discrete elements don't know how to make themselves visible.

WILLIAM H.

All simulacra reflected in mirrors, since they present the exact appearance of objects, can only be images detached from surfaces. For every object, there is a precise subtle reproduction. Its individual elements are invisible, but through the impetus of a mirror, which constantly returns it, the whole may appear before our eyes.

DENNIS PS.

Images are but the tatters of our dress of light, whole within us, as we are whole within it.

M. GOODMAN.

These images, these simulacra, these tatters, figures, angels – are they light, are they bodies?

LEWIS DE B.

I'd like to ask our philosopher (as well as our friend William, who seems to agree), if these images only emanate from their objects when there's somebody there to see them, or if these simulacra pour forth even when nobody's looking. If he leans toward the first hypothesis, I'd like to ask him what force puts these simulacra so thoroughly at the disposal of the onlooker, and so deftly that whenever he turns his head, they turn as well.

LEWIS DE B.

If he favors the second proposition, which is to say, if he maintains that simulacra continually flow out of all things, then I'd like to ask how long their elements hold together, given that there's no physical link binding them. And if we come to the conclusion that these simulacra do remain intact, how do they hold any heat? For nature, even when bodiless, cannot exist without a body. Next, how could anyone believe that wherever you turn your gaze, images will rush up to meet it, images of sky, earth, streams, fields, ships, herds, and everything else that we see in a glance, especially given the tiny size of the pupil that drinks it all in? How could you ever see a whole army? Do the simulacra coming off of each soldier recombine, take their place, and then penetrate the spectator's eye?

BASIL OF C.

The sun, having absorbed light, holds it tangled in its own substance and will not let go, while the moon constantly sheds its clothes of light, then dresses itself again.

M. GOODMAN.

Who could skin light from luminous bodies?

JOHN PH.

If all air were filled with the traveling images of objects, wouldn't we be able to see what's behind our backs?

DENNIS PS.

Simulacra are Demons, endless emanations of the goddess Rhea.

WILLIAM H.

When the Heavens are veiled in darkest night
    On that same field where the battle once waged
    One sees again airy shadows clash mid-flight,
    'Tis the noble dead crashing down a confused lane.
In well-ordered rows horses and men
    Seem to extend their many burdened hands through air
    Whipping the troops round again
    On this deserted ground.

WILLIAM H.

Who are these figures? Is the courage of the dead
    Emblazoned with such hatred and such fury?
      Or do these weird Demons
Draw close to this city
      As of old they appeared at Achilles' grave,
      Frolicking to fool our gaze?

LEWIS DE B.

Light is everywhere contained and diffused in matter; its mere presence gives birth to images. But the change that takes place when light is diffused through matter is caused by matter, and not by light itself, by the gathering of sunlight when it's mixed with cloud, or a fine white cloth screened by a dark body, for the darkness is hidden by an abundance of darkness, or by the gathering light as it cuts through three windows – the second pane receives less light than the first, and the third less than the second. Clearly, this is not due to light's weakness, but to the panes that block its path, for light carries rough bodies.

DENNIS PS.

Facing the source of Light stand the Barzakhs, the screens, the dividers – these are body itself, and pure shadow. They would persist, unaltered, even if light retreated. The body in itself, when related to light, is absolute Negativity. But light is essentially present to itself; it is the revelation of the self to the self. It has no need, no way of knowing itself outside itself.

Remember Iblis's sin, fleeing light, believing he could see by his own light.

JOHN PH.

Light leads the eye beyond the where.

M. GOODMAN.

But how? Is light continuous in simultaneity as well as in sequence? I'd like to know what you think about this.

M. GOODMAN.

Let's begin with the notion that the point of a cone formed by visual rays is not completely and evenly filled with rays. Instead, any two neighboring rays are separated by an angle that, though extremely small, still exists. Although the separation between angles starts out so small, if you take the lines along a straight path, the distance between them must, given the laws of geometry, grow. We thereby understand the fundamental fact of all perspective: distant objects disappear because they fall into the black space between two contiguous rays.

WILLIAM H.

Shadow is the wake of a ray of light.

JOHN PH.

As you know, some people have claimed that light, whether it moves in a straight line or not, travels from the eye toward the mirror and not from the mirror to the eye. But in any case, all these problems can be solved by the concept of *energeia*. And what's more, this concept unites the idea of light-as-wave with that of light-as-particle.

LEWIS DE B.

To say that light moves in a straight line is only a convenient way of speaking.

BASIL OF C.

In the divinely illuminated air, what should we believe? That air, viewed as air, is also light, or that, viewed as light, it is also air? In reality, the word is clear; air is not really light, nor light air, but air is in the light and light is in the air.

54

Perhaps you're not far from the crux of the matter this time. It's true that air lit by the sun suddenly seems to be light and nothing but light, not because it loses its own nature but because light is so dominant that the air is filled with it.

Just so, human nature united with God can be considered entirely God, not because it's no longer imperfect, but because it has become so saturated with the divine that only God remains visible. Air without light is dark, but sunlight can be seen apart from any bodily manifestation, existing in and of itself. And when the sun's rays mix with air and melt in it, air, imperceptible by itself, can be seen through this fusion.

M. GOODMAN

If I understand you correctly, you're saying that just as air appears to be entirely light, melting gold appears to be entirely fire, even though their substances (in themselves non-luminous) are not obliterated by that contact. And so it follows that any natural element, corporeal or incorporeal, becomes visible because in the end it must unite with God, the divinity in and beyond?

BASIL OF C.

There is no rest for air until it is wholly loved by light, until it is contained in this whole and fully understands it. Tiny particles of air can choose to reach the entirety of non-dust in the whole that is 55 circumscribed by light.

WILLIAM H.

How by mine eyes could such a grand
lady enter, small as they are?
And how is it she remains in mine heart
that carries her in it wherever it travels?
   That place where she enters no one may see
And strikes me with wonder
But I aim to absorb her in light
My gaze on the glass where she lingers.
   The trapped fire soon sends out
Its flames still without breaking
Thus through mine eyes does come to heart
   Not the woman but her image
I long to be renewed in a love
Marked by such a creature's symbol.

LEWIS DE B.

The concept of a punctiform ray has long been a problem, driving many physicists to distraction: how to thread the little needle of the eye with images of large, luminous camels?

JOHN PH.

From the point of view of common sense, the way light is said to act is absurd, but it matches experience perfectly. We must accept light as it is: from all these absurd points of view.

FIFTH NIGHT

DENNIS PS.

Seen from above, from our terrace tonight, the illuminated city straddling the river spreads out at our feet in all its glimmering splendor. Just imagine how dark it must seem up here, from the teeming streets below. From down there, to the most distant light in the procession, the brightest light up here is the most dispersed, the most particulate, diluted, the darkest. From up here, contemplating the Seraphim, for example, the most prominent light is that which is most concentrated, the simplest, most universal, the one that best maintains the unity, vigor, and radiance of its source.

LEWIS DE B.

The lampyris, commonly called a glow-worm, that lowly insect that dimly shines in the shadows of summer nights, that diamond in the grass, beats all lighting records when it comes to sheer output. Though the light it emits is rather weak, it's entirely concentrated within the visible spectrum, so all the energy it puts out manifests as visible light.

M. GOODMAN

This house was built by my maternal grandfather (my mother was an Olbers). He converted the upper floors into an observatory and dedicated the greater part of his evenings to astronomy, particularly

to comets and minor planets. My grandfather was, like Mr. Pickwick
(the hero of his favorite book, which he re-read every other year), a
perfect example of what the English used to call a "natural philosopher"
(though he had little interest in the German philosophy of nature).
He was passionate about the classification of clouds (and the com-
parative merits of Lamarck's system as compared to our own, which
comes to us from a Quaker pharmacist, Luke Howard), but above
all, he reflected on this difficult question: why is the night sky black?

WILLIAM H.

Thou black, in whom all colors are comprised,
    And to whom all in the end return
    You, color, of sun there where it burns,
Shadow where it cools; all
That Nature proposes is locked in you, or disposed
    In other colors: from you do arise
Those humors and complexions which, disclosed
    Through you, do work as mysteries
Of that your hidden power; when you reign,
    Fortune's letters shine in the skies
To tell us what the Heavens do ordain:
    But when the common glow of earth shines in our eyes,
You pull back in disdain
    All revelation to man denied.

BASIL OF C.

How could the Night Sky not be black? Stars shine there, indestructible, the eternal houses of God, but between them lie the immense fields of darkness.

JOHN PH.

You allot this patchwork of alternating dark and light, these fields, those celestial meadows of grazing stars, to the gods, but that in no way proves that the heavenly vault is indestructible.

JOHN PH.

Those who believe that churches and temples are full of the Gods' spirits and who raise their hands in supplication don't think these dwellings without beginning or definite end.

DENNIS PS.

The nature of light is essentially cursive, protean, even contradictory. Depending on whether it's considered in a positive or negative context, the same luminous field could just as well appear as absolute darkness or shining brilliance.

BASIL OF C.

Consider this absurdity: the sun and stars are light, and the Sun of all suns is even more light.

LEWIS DE B.

But that's not the question Mr. Goodman's asking (the one that consumed his grandfather). Why is the background of the night sky black? Reason would seem to argue against it.

WILLIAM H.

            Night, that
    reverend black
                shock of hair light is just
                there to define it
                thus
        the first night preceded day

M. GOODMAN

This is how he reasoned (I'm speaking of my grandfather, in his astronomical considerations): let us accept the cosmological principle (that the universe, with the exception of purely local irregularities such as galaxies, everywhere presents the same face).

Let's imagine a very large spherical shell with an arbitrary center, a radius of r, and a thickness (almost infinitely small compared to the radius) of dr. We'll assume that the sphere's volume (4 pi r squared dr) is large enough for the light emitted by the stars within it to equal its volume (according to the formula) multiplied by U when U is the product of the average number of stars in a unit of volume times the average luminosity of a star (the notion of "average" making sense in light of the cosmological principle as long as everything is considered on a large enough scale). Do you follow me?

JOHN PH.

I precede you: the luminosity of the stars at the center of the shell universe you have imagined—this terrace for example—is consequently Udr and is therefore effectively independent of the sphere's radius.

WILLIAM H.

Which means you take the following to be true:
Condition i: the average density and the average luminosity of stars do not vary over time.

DENNIS PS.

And condition II: nor do their numbers vary over time.

And your grandfather, I presume, took condition III to be true: space is Euclidian, but even if one assumes Lobatchevskian space, the result would be the same, wouldn't it?

BASIL OF C.

I agree. And then we have condition IV: physical laws apply everywhere in space, and not only on our particular globe. God wished it so.

BASIL OF C.

But we also have to include condition V, which is essential to your grandfather's reasoning: stars don't move in groups.

M. GOODMAN

Right.

LEWIS DE B.

You could follow this reasoning out to the conclusion that so troubled your grandfather: if the luminosity of the stars at the center of this hypothetical shell is fixed, and we then surround this shell, onion-style, with other shells of equal thickness, concentric to the first, making the exterior limit of one the interior surface of the next, each shell will then contribute equally to the central radiation. And since we can keep adding shells to our first imaginary sphere, the radiation's density would itself be infinite. Heaven would be full of infinite light.

JOHN PH.

Couldn't we imagine a thin gas that absorbs radiation?

DENNIS PS.

Or that light is, in fact, infinite, but that we're blind to it?

WILLIAM H.

glory throwing light on all inner
regions of the divine
mind sight
stops at the casement

WILLIAM H.

and in vain
folds back
to its own
inside

BASIL OF C.

Isn't that proof of supernatural intervention?

DENNIS PS.

Infinite light is, precisely, black.

M. GOODMAN

My grandfather prosaically supposed that Hubble was right and condition V was wrong: the universe is expanding.

JOHN PH.

Why not get rid of IV, too: physical laws are strictly local.

LEWIS DE B.

Be serious.

LEWIS DE B.

Let's work from the assumption that physical laws are universal, and that the cosmological principle holds. And it's just not conceivable that the universe is simply "young." So Hubble's hypothesis stands, and has been proved many times – though I applaud your grandfather's perspicacity.

JOHN PH.

65

I second your suggestion.

BASIL OF C.

Let's give thanks to God who gives us light, and let us honor Mr. Goodman's grandfather.

M. GOODMAN

Thank you.

DENNIS PS.

Night is getting on. It's time to stop, for sleep, or further contemplation.

SIXTH NIGHT

LEWIS DE B.

Light is made of drops, like drops of rain (drops of light are photons);
when light is a single color, all the drops are the same size.

M. GOODMAN

I like that comparison.

WILLIAM H.

The wall the leaves parted *yellow* on the wall
the leaves parted *under the yellow*   SUN the
wall Of leaves parted *of yellow*   OF SUN
the wall The leaves parted *yellow*   SUN the
wall The leaves parted   *yellow* on the wall The
leaves parted *under the yellow*   SUN the wall
Of leaves parted *of yellow*   OF SUN the
wall the leaves parted   *yellow*   SUN

The wall The leaves *the yellow parted*   SUN

BASIL OF C.

The rain just stopped, and in the evening, at the moment of giving us back the *yellow* SUN God filled the sky and our eyes with a bracelet of color. For our last night, it seems right that we should discuss its composition and properties, and therefore, its meaning. We've all prepared for this, as agreed, by thoroughly studying the terrestrial and heavenly phenomenon of the rainbow.

JOHN PH.

It's clear that the rainbow belongs to a family of 15 distinct kinds of radiant impression:

    I   the primary rainbow
    II   the white cloud at the center of I
    III the dark cloud around I
    IV the secondary rainbow (above I)
    V   the secondary white cloud surrounding IV
    VI the white arc immersed in transparent fog
    VII the red arc
    VIII the large solar halo
    IX the solar column
    X   the lunar column
    XI the red halo that surrounds the sun, moon, or brilliant stars
    XII the smaller solar halo that parallels VIII but whose colors run in the opposite order
    XIII the luminous rays (virgae) at the edges of dense clouds
    XIV the parahelia on each side of the sun
    XV the colors of stars seen in haze

DENNIS PS.

The following colors are Acts of Light:
- white light is visualized light
- yellow light is loyalized light
- dark blue light is benevolent light
- green light is that of the soul at peace

DENNIS PS.

But *Black Light* is missing, the light of passionate love.

LEWIS DE B.

The rainbow shows us that our sense of sight is informed by four colors: Red, yellow, green, and blue. I agree with Theodoric of Freiberg. Aristotle acknowledges only three of these colors, but Theodoric, quite rightly, differs from his master on this point; furthermore, he says (and again, I agree) "the same learned philosopher tells us that we should never drift far from what the gifts of our senses make abundantly clear."

JOHN PH.

And let's not forget that there are many other types of rainbows besides the one the sun shows us as it peeks out through the rain over the river and the city:

- that made by the sun's rays cutting through dewdrops hanging off a spider's web at dawn
- that born of the same dew scattered across grass and seen at just the right angle
- that of the prism

M. GOODMAN

You're leaving out the one the sun's rays cast in the slender jet of water that hurdles through air toward the day-star, which we see as we stand in the shade of the plane trees in front of the café.

BASIL OF C.

Each of these is equally worthy of our attention, like all things created and beautiful.

WILLIAM H.

Colors are the vowels of the rainbow's language.

WILLIAM H.

The rainbow, Jean Philopon also says, perfumes the view.

DENNIS PS.

In the rainbow of prose, green light indicates mystery, but it's black light that heralds enigma. It's also there in the sky's rainbow, and in all things – in their presence, their appearance, and their absence, it intervenes as purely dazzling essence.

BASIL OF C.

The rainbow is proof of light; as such, a lesson in divinity is inscribed in its every aspect.

LEWIS DE B.

The rainbow
  – a glittering event produced by luminous rays springing from an illuminated celestial body, refracted twice and reflected once inward through spherical drops of rain or dew.

M. GOODMAN

  – is born of a specific point directly across a luminous body from the observer, such that the angles of incidence and reflection are equal in relation to star and observer.

JOHN PH.

– is made by rays slicing the surface of each drop into three invariable points (determined by nature), creating regions from which colors shine forth.

JOHN PH.

– extends itself in an arc subtended by a 22-degree angle in the eye of the observer, highest when the sun is at the horizon and inversely proportional to the sun's height above the horizon.

WILLIAM H.

– is composed of bands of color that occupy an area corresponding to the surface area of the drops from which they shine.

M. GOODMAN

– reflected from flocks of droplets floating at different altitudes and arranged within a space (not a point) such that the flock's most elevated and highest droplets refract along the largest angle and shoot back out at various angles of reflection.

DENNIS PS.

– projected so that if the color red strikes the observer's eye from the highest drops, the other colors from these drops will be thrown behind him, while a drop from the lower part of the herd will produce the red in front, the yellow in his eye, and the blue and green behind him.

LEWIS DE B.

– arranged so that the observer sees red at the top of the arc, then yellow below, then green, and finally blue closest to the arc's center.

BASIL OF C.

– varies according to the observer's position and thus moves when he moves.

BASIL OF C.

– is produced by rays that appear at the intersection of a path that turns around a point on the horizon directly facing the observer.

JOHN PH.

– always occupies some portion of a circle.

- is produced by rays set on one side of an isosceles triangle, which, in projecting itself onto the horizon, loses five-sixtieths of its length.

WILLIAM H.

- is positioned at fifty-five sixtieths of the distance from the observer's eye to the horizon when the sun is standing opposite.

DENNIS PS.

- is positioned on a circle that forms the base of a cone whose summit is the sun and whose axis passes through the observer's eye.

M. GOODMAN

- a perfect half-circle when the sun is on the horizon.

M. GOODMAN

- less than a half-circle when the sun is above, the arc's center thrusting over the horizon at an angle that equals that of the sun's elevation.

BASIL OF C.

– such that the center of the circle of which it is an arc is always on the straight line that links the observer's eye to the sun.

DENNIS PS.

– is surrounded by an unclouded area tending toward white between the horizon and the concavity of the arc.

JOHN PH.

– so that no more light reflects above.

WILLIAM H.

– is surrounded by a lightless region tending toward black above the convexity of the arc.

LEWIS DE B.

But no one can explain, in this case and others (such as when an electron swims back up the stream of time, traveling "counter-time" to absorb a photon, then starts off again in time's direction), why light acts like this and not like that. Its moves are so quick, so slick, we'll never divine its method. No one can track it, and I certainly can't grasp it.

FINAL

Here these *exchanges on light* come to a close.

I thank each of my partners in these is six dialogues. They modestly did not wish their names to be revealed except as abbreviations from which, nonetheless, their identities are easily decipherable.

I also thank all those who, without having directly taken part in our conversations, have in one manner or another enriched our reflections; among these I would particularly like to name:

Monsieur and Madame Proclus, Iamblichus, Pseudo-Dionysius, Aristotle, Alhazen, Hussayn, Ibn Ishaq, Hooke, Newton, Pythagoras, Euclid, Lord Kelvin, Grosseteste, Cavalcanti, Marino, St. Ambrose, St. John of Damascus, Guy le Fèvre de La Boderie, Giacomo da Lentini, Ulric of Strasbourg, Al-Farabi, Ludwig Wittgenstein, Denis Roche, Suhrawardi, Avicebrol, Sylvia Townsend Warner, J.J. Thomson, Democritus, Anaximenes, Anaximander, Empedocles, Heron of Alexandria, Macrobius, Lucretius, Roger Bacon, René Descartes, Damianus, Saint Augustine, Jean de Buridan, Feynman, and Theodoric of Freiberg.

ACKNOWLEDGEMENTS

Portions of this translation have appeared in *Drunken Boat, kadar koli, Provincetown Arts,* and *Verse,* and as a chapbook published by Beard of Bees. Many thanks to the editors of these. And many, many thanks to Jean-Jacques Poucel, who contributed so greatly to this translation, and to both Warren Motte and Jennifer Papp for key clarifications.

Jacques Roubaud is one of France's leading contemporary writers. Working in poetry, fiction, essay, and theater, his voice ranges from crisp analysis to dashing humor to delicate and anchored emotion. A prominent member of the Oulipo (the Workshop for Potential Literature), he taught mathematics for many years at the Université de Paris X. He has also published critical works on the alexandrine and on the troubadour poets as well as an examination of contemporary poetry, *Poésie, etcetera: ménage*, which is available in an English translation by Guy Bennett from Green Integer Books. Roubaud is also a prolific translator from Japanese and English, including such classics as Lewis Carroll's *The Hunting of the Snark*. His work has been widely translated, and many of his books, including *The Great Fire of London, Some Thing Black,* and *The Form of a City Changes Faster, Alas, Than the Human Heart* are available in English through Dalkey Archive Press. A book-length critical analysis of his work, *Jacques Roubaud and the Invention of Memory* by Jean-Jacques Poucel, is available from the University of North Carolina Press.

Eleni Sikelianos is the author of several books, most recently the volumes of poetry *Body Clock* and *The California Poem,* published by Coffee House Press, and a memoir *The Book of Jon,* published by City Lights. Her awards include a Fulbright Fellowship to Greece and the Seeger Fellowship at Princeton as well as an NEA and a National Poetry Series selection for her book *The Monster Lives of Boys and Girls.* She translates from both Greek and French, and currently teaches in the Ph.D. program in creative writing at the University of Denver.

This is the fourth title in the La Presse series of contemporary French poetry in translation. The cover image is a page from the original Éditions A.M. Métailié publication with holographic notes made by the translator. This series is edited by Cole Swensen and designed by Shari DeGraw. This book is set in Sumner Stone's Magma. BookMobile of Minneapolis printed and bound the edition.